MW01267970

GO FEARLESS

FIRST EDITION

10 POWERFUL SECRETS TO HELP YOU INCREASE YOUR CONFIDENCE, START TAKING ACTION, AND ACHIEVE WHATEVER YOU WANT IN LIFE

NATE LEE MORALES

TheSTRIVE.co

Printed in the United States of America

CATALOG:
Morales, Nate Lee

    Go Fearless/Nate Lee Morales
p. cm.

First Edition
Interior Designed by: Strive Industries, LLC

THE STRIVE.co
Strive Industries LLC.

DEDICATION 🔥

This resource is dedicated to my two children, Mason and Madison, and my loving wife Jessica. You are my inspiration for everything I do, and every decision I make.

I'd also like to dedicate this book to my mom, who always urged me to follow my heart. Last but certainly not least, I'd like to dedicate this book to you and everyone else who has a desire to unleash their unique spark into the world and to live life fully.

GO FEARLESS

TABLE OF CONTENTS:

INTRODUCTION

"MEN ARE ANXIOUS TO IMPROVE THEIR CIRCUMSTANCES, BUT ARE UNWILLING TO IMPROVE THEMSELVES: THEY THEREFORE REMAIN BOUND."

- JAMES ALLEN -

The quote above is a phenomenon that I've observed all too often throughout my life.

I always hear people say they want to get better, want to do more, become more, improve their lives, change; but at the end of the day, most people never take the consistent steps necessary to get the changes they envisioned for themselves.

From years of study and research, I've concluded, that much of this phenomenon can be attributed to our human nature. It's natural to feel resistance to improvement, to growth. The bird gets the resistance of gravity when it attempts to fly. The flower gets resistance from nearby plants trying to crowd out its space as it reaches up to capture its moment in the sun.

"THE SECRET TO HAPPINESS IS FREEDOM...AND THE SECRET TO FREEDOM IS COURAGE."

- THUCYDIDES -

What I want to suggest to you is that resistance is natural, but succumbing to it, is not. Fear, much like resistance, is nothing but the human motive of aversion.[1]

Because you are reading this, I am going to take a wild guess, and assume you want more for your life. I am sure you want to grow, to become that ideal version of yourself which you have envisioned in your heart. I can confidently say, that you, like everyone else, also have a resistance trying to keep you from changing, from growing, from doing what you deep down inside, truly desire to be doing.

As such, I am respectfully suggesting to you, to push, to strive, to break yourself free from the shackles of habit and aversion. I am asking you to commit to pursuing the new you that is bound to come forth from conquering those fears and doubts which hold all too many of us back.

The fears and doubts that keep the majority of people living out their lives in quiet desperation, only to go to their graves with their gifts, dreams, talents, and aspirations left inside them.

In the next section I am going to tell you a brief story about myself as it relates to lack of confidence and fear, and why I decided to create this resource for you. I'll then, give you some of the secrets I've used to boost my belief in myself and increase my confidence; allowing me to face my challenges fearlessly, and gain the courage to live the life that I truly wanted for myself, rather than doing what others wanted of me.

> **"THOSE WHO TAKE UP ANY SUBJECT WITH AN OPEN MIND, WILLING TO LEARN ANYTHING THAT WILL CONTRIBUTE TO THEIR ADVANCEMENT, COMFORT, AND HAPPINESS, ARE WISE."**
>
> **- JOHN MCDONALD -**

With great respect,

NATE LEE MORALES

A SHORT STORY

Many of those who know me would describe me as confident, gregarious, outgoing, and those really closest to me, would probably describe me as fearless.

What my friends, family, and those in my closest circles know about me, is a public result that stems from countless victories I have created in private.

What the people closest to me have never seen, or are unaware of, are the internal battles and mental struggles I've had to go through to 'show up' as the confident person they've come to know and respect. Behind the scenes, I am as fragile, sensitive, and vulnerable as any other person.

Behind the scenes, out of the public eye, I am all too human. I am a very real person, who is faced with significant choices that need to be made on a daily basis, just like you.

Many of these choices are comprised of an option to either shirk opportunities for growth and expansion, or lean in to face them fearlessly with full acceptance of the outcome.

When I was younger, I played both High School football and NCAA Division I football, and I had a reputation for being fearless. To some of my peers I was known as "Stixx", a name affectionately attributed to me while playing Strong Safety. It was a name I was given because of my penchant for "Sticking" my opponents on the field; in other words, hitting the other guys ridiculously hard. I had zero fears of my opponents, regardless of their size or reputation.

In other circles, I was known as "Captain Kaboom" or "Captain Crash", for my intrepid, border-line dangerous performances on special teams. You see, when I played special teams I was what is known as a 'wedge-buster'. On special teams I was essentially the guy who was responsible for running down the field at full speed after a kick off, and tasked with 'busting the wedge'.

Essentially this equates to a person smashing into a wall of four or five big, mean, tough defenders, clustering together to protect the kick returner from getting tackled or hurt.

To help you imagine what this looks like, just think of a bowling ball flying down the lanes and blasting apart a bunch of bowling pins. Yes, I was the bowling ball.

I relay this story to you in detail because I WAS what many would call fearless. I was not afraid of anything or anyone, especially when it came to sports. I am sure most of that courage and confidence stemmed from the emotional and mental state many of us experience in our youth. Regardless of where it may have come from, all I know, is I had it. I was Fearless.

Oddly though, something happened to me over the years, something had certainly changed in me. You see, once I graduated from college and entered the proverbial working world, the seemingly impenetrable confidence that I had in my youth seemed to vanish almost overnight.

Early on, I couldn't put a finger on why I had lost that fearlessness I once had, or where it went, all I knew was that it was gone.

The fear and doubt that I started to have was real. Right before I started my first job out of college, I had some of the biggest doubts of my life. I didn't believe myself to be worthy of the job I was just offered, and was straight out scared to take it. Before I accepted the offer, I actually had to reach out to my mother, and get her to reaffirm that I did deserve the job, and that I could do it. My fear and doubt was so great, that I needed external permission to make what now seems like a simple career choice.

Fortunately for me, I took the job. Unfortunately; the fear, doubt, and lack of confidence didn't stop.

After a couple of years on that first job, I decided to leave because I didn't feel confident about the work I was doing, regardless of being trained on the subject over the past four years. In general, I didn't feel confident about my life, or my place in it.

So I changed jobs, and moved to another city hoping the fear and doubt would subside. Still nothing changed. The fear, doubt, and insecurity were still there. In fact, it was stronger than ever before.

After about four grueling years had passed, I decided that I had to find a way to live in a more positive, hopeful, and confident way. I decided that I had to get rid of those nagging feelings of doubt. I had to get rid of this fear that seemed to follow me in just about all my undertakings.

As such, I made the choice to do two things. On one hand, I decided to proactively seek out solutions as to why I was feeling so defeated, so lacking in courage, so full of fear.

I began reading tons of books, listening to hours and hours of audio books, and experimenting with a whole bunch of different things, (meditation, affirmations, guided visualizations, hypnosis etc.) just to see what worked.

On the other hand, I decided to leave my cushy Analyst job working for a boutique engineering firm, and thrust myself into an industry which I knew nothing about. In essence, I decided to face my fears head on. I decided to pursue what I felt I had to do, regardless of the disapproval and admonishments from the many well-meaning, but dead wrong external voices (friends, family, society, etc.).

Miraculously, the fear and uneasiness that I was always caring around in my gut, **seemed** to slowly abate. My courage began to eventually come back; I started to feel as if I was ready to take on the world once again. In short, **I came back to life**.

Fortunately for me, I have not looked back since those very gray and uncertain days. I've been moving forward fearlessly ever since. And with each year that passes, life seems to get better, brighter, and filled with more promise.

After doing some deep thinking on how I came to resuscitate my confidence and courage to live life fully and on my own terms; I came up with was a handful of practices that I believe primed me to take the action I most needed to take.

These practices are what I've used in the past, and make up the bulk of the formula that I am now about to share with you.

In short, the insights I am providing in this resource for you, are the culmination of those particular tools and strategies I researched and tested on myself, which worked best for me.

If I were to pinpoint the one act that made the biggest impact on how I felt, it would have been the act of courageously following my heart.   But, I may have never gotten to that point, without first utilizing the all the secrets mentioned in this book.

I am confident, that if you attempt to conquer your fear using the insights provided in this book with full faith, and with complete commitment, you will eventually experience noticeable progress in your self-belief, confidence, and your ability to defeat your fears.

It must also be noted, that through all my experiences, fear has always been there. It may have appeared as if it was gone from time to time, but it was still there. In fact, it still is, especially when I am stretching myself to do things I've never done before. Some fears are just as present today as they were when I got started on my personal journey of personal growth and change.

The primary difference between then and now; is I have the tools at my disposal to put fear in its place, and the steadfastness to implement them, especially when fear tries to get the best of me.

One of the biggest obstacles of my successes in the past was self-doubt and a lack of confidence, which created a real FEAR of failure. Ever since I learned how to increase my ability to be fearless, my achievements and successes in life have increased at an accelerated rate. In fact, I've noticed that the level of my successes (and happiness) have been almost directly proportional to the degree in which I have conquered my self-limiting beliefs.

The more I worked on diminishing my self-doubt and increasing my confidence, the more fearless I became. And the more fearless I became, the easier it became to succeed in all departments of my life.

The motivation behind the creation of this resource stems from my observations (and personal experience) that one of the biggest things keeping us from truly living an extraordinary life, and from succeeding at our highest levels, is fear.

I created this resource to help you conquer your fears, and to add value to you by saving you the extraordinary time investment, money investment, and emotional investment I had to make to learn these many lessons myself.

In essence, I want to help you conquer your fears as soon as possible. I want you to become more successful now (if you so choose), rather than later, because life is too short, and because your greatest life demands it.

I want to help you **gain the courage to live the life you want**, rather than doing what others want of you.

What many of us don't realize, is how big of an impact fear plays on how our lives turn out. We don't realize that fear can really limit us in living a happy fulfilled life. It can keep us from success, it can keep us from becoming our best self. It can keep us from living a truly extraordinary life.

For instance, fear can keep us from applying for that dream job that we've always wanted, or it can hinder our ability to take action on starting that big potentially life-changing project we have wanted to launch. Fear can even keep us from approaching and thus finding our one true love, our soulmate. Fear can really interfere with our doing a whole lot of things. Fear has the power to limit our life.

I found a quote in a book I read, where the late Wayne Dyer stated, "The number one regret of the dying is 'I wish I had the courage to live the life I wanted rather than doing what others wanted of me.'"

If there was one true aim of my efforts, and this resource, is to help you avoid that regret. I want to help you avoid, years from now, when you are on your deathbed, uttering the words:

"I wish I had trusted my gut, I should have done what I truly wanted, I wish I would have been more fearless."

If we let it, fear will sabotage our biggest plans, it will snuff our highest hopes. Fear will stop us from living the life we were meant to live. It can, and it will keep us from living our greatest life, unless...

We decide to conquer it!

Let's begin our conquest my friend, let's **Go Fearless**! Are you ready?

HOW TO USE THE GO FEARLESS BOOK

This resource is a collection of the most effective courage boosting **secrets** I've gathered and used myself over the years.

When these secret antidotes are successfully weaved together, they produce an effective "formula" that will help you feel more confident, have a stronger belief in yourself, allowing you to become fearless and start taking action to achieve more in your life.

antidote

noun | an·ti·dote | \ˈan-ti-ˌdōt\

Definition of ANTIDOTE FOR ENGLISH LANGUAGE LEARNERS

: a substance that stops the harmful effects of a poison

: something that corrects or improves the bad effects of something

For first time use, I highly recommend reading through the book in its entirety. After you have conducted an initial review and deep consideration of every concept contained within it, then decide to choose those aspects (antidotes) that resonated with you the most, or that made you feel the most at ease, **the most fearless**.

At this point, you will have created a formula that works best for you.

Study your "Go Fearless" formula on a daily basis to strengthen your fearless muscles. By doing this, you will slowly create the confidence and fearlessness needed to take on those seemingly daunting challenges within your life. It is highly recommended that you review the formula in a ritualized manner. If you can commit to reviewing it for at least 66 days, you will ingrain your new fearlessness as a habit.

If you are not sure where you will find the time to implement these antidotes, I highly recommend you either wake up 30 minutes earlier each day, or schedule in the time during lunch breaks, or even right before you go to bed. The important thing is that you actively make time to practice the antidotes.

As the saying goes, what gets scheduled gets done. So it's vital to make time for exercising the mental muscles that will allow you to become fearless.

By approaching your fears in a systematic way, you will be empowering yourself to take on your challenges with much more conviction, confidence, and courage. In effect, you will increase your ability to successfully confront your challenges/situations, while minimizing the fear normally experienced when pushing through such activities.

Lastly, I am not the expert. I just have my experiences and my results. I am simply the alchemist, the illuminator, the guide. It's time to go fearless my friend.

ANTIDOTE 1: THE LIFE ENHANCEMENT PROCESS

THE FOUNDATION:

This first antidote consists of one process, but illustrated in two different ways. The two diagrams are meant to inform you, as well as act as an incentive to encourage you to continue using the other 9 antidotes.

Both of these diagrams are important to comprehend, but the diagram that is best to keep in mind as you utilize the other antidotes to create your fearless formula, is this first one, *Diagram 1*. I suggest that it is kept at the forefront of your mind, and used as a foundation as you strengthen your fearless muscles. I recommend this because of the substantial life enhancing effects that can result from you **believing** that you can become fearless.

Without further ado, here is the first diagram, your foundation, and your strong reason as to why you should become fearless.

DIAGRAM 1: This diagram (see on next page) is a model for life enhancement. When we comprehend how this model impacts our life, we can equip ourselves with the conviction that is needed to jumpstart our intentions for facing our fears.

The model demonstrates how you can actually **decide** to crush your fears, and take steps to continually suppress those fears, while at the same time setting yourself up for future success.

When you observe the model on the next page you will notice that it is cyclical. You should also take note, that the model spirals in a direction that is toward a stronger, increasingly improved you, which naturally translates into a brighter future for you.

You'll notice when looking at this model (especially in comparison to the second diagram provided just after this one) the word **'Increased'**.

This entire model is impacted by the decision to **increase our belief** that we can become fearless, and an increase in our belief of ourselves. As a result, a bigger brighter, more fulfilled future can ensue.

The premise of the model is this: If you force yourself to have certainty about your abilities, an absolute belief that you can handle whatever it is you are undertaking, you will place in motion a positive life enhancing process.

When you decide to increase your belief that you can do something, you will influence your potential for actually being able to do that thing well.

Having the sense that you have increased potential to accomplish something, you will in effect be more likely to take (increased) action to fulfill that potential. As you begin taking more action, and doing so with full faith in your potential and ability to execute flawlessly, you will begin to get better results.

Having these improved results will reinforce your belief in yourself, and in your abilities. In turn, the whole process will restart anew, and every recurring time, it will be from an even stronger, more confident position.

In summary: with a decision to believe in one's self, one's potential to execute will increase. Consequently, one will be inclined to take even more action, whereby, one will inevitably see more improved results. As time goes on, this process will compound all results. Therefore, it is vital to begin from a position of belief, to get onto the path towards living fearlessly.

DIAGRAM 2: Diagram 2 is very similar to Diagram 1, just illustrated above. This diagram was included primarily to provide additional context in relation to the power of belief. Its purpose is to demonstrate what the opposite effects are, if we get started on the wrong foot.

This diagram, unlike Diagram 1, is on a negative spiraling path towards a diminishing life. It is different in that it consists of a cycle of decrease. In essence, when we allow for things, people, or our own negative opinion of ourselves to **negatively impact** our belief in ourselves and our abilities, we will inevitably experience a level of diminishment in our potential. Through this feeling of diminished capabilities, we will in effect act less on the fulfillment of our goals. Like most people, when something seems futile, we are less inclined to persevere. As a perfect example of cause and effect, our lack of action (or our half-hearted action) leads to substandard results.

And the cycle goes on. Those less than stellar results reinforce our lack of belief in ourselves (again), which as a result decreases our outlook on our potential even more so. In turn, this ultimately reduces even further, our desire to act, yet again bringing even worse results, etc.

This phase can go on indefinitely to eventual physical, spiritual, and professional defeat. Something I do not want for you, or anyone.

The most critical aspect to take away from this antidote (considering both diagrams), is that it is critical that we start all of our undertakings from a place of belief.

If you, as you go through these additional antidotes, start having any doubts, or begin to feel your inner cynic start to come out, just come back to antidote 1 and review and reacquaint until you are ready to move forward with faith.

Remember, it is important to believe that you can learn how to become more confident. It is important to believe that you can do amazing things, and it's essential that you believe you can become a fearless version of your former self.

"IF YOU MUST DOUBT SOMETHING, DOUBT YOUR LIMITS."

- PRICE PRITCHETT -

ANTIDOTE 2: SIX TRUTHS ABOUT FEAR

Below are six very important truths that when deeply understood, can assist you in the easing of your apprehensions. [2]

I suggest you attempt to internalize these truths. By doing so, you will be conditioning your mind to release the stress that you may have built up around your fears in the past.

1. Fear never goes away, as long as we are growing, stretching, and striving for more. Fear then, is but a natural consequence of striving.

2. To start feeling confident and good about ourselves, we have to take some type of definitive steps/actions to improve the situation or ourselves.

3. The only way to get rid of the fear of doing something is to go out and do that thing which we fear.

4. Fear is something that is experienced by everyone. To be human, is to fear. Fear is a natural byproduct of growth; it's a byproduct of placing ourselves in unfamiliar territory,

outside of our comfort zones. We are all human, and thus we all experience fear.

5. Living with the regret and the feeling of helplessness the stems from not tackling your fears is more frightening than having decided to face your fears head on.

6. The more attention we give to our fears without doing something to combat them, the stronger they will grow, and the more paralyzed you'll feel when you decide to conquer them.

I've experienced best results when reading these five truths out loud whenever fear begins to creep up in our mind.

The simple act of reading these out lout can have a strong effect in disarming the paralyzing effects that fear can have on us.

It's like preparing for a big game or battle against a worthy opponent. The more you know about your opponent, the less frightening it is. The less frightening the opponent appears, the more willing we are to face it.

ANTIDOTE 3: THE SIX ACTIONS FOR CURING FEAR

H ere are six practical actions that I've successfully tested with great results. [3] These guidelines will be helpful to keep in your 'back pocket' so-to-speak, so they can be easily accessed when the time comes for proactively curing your fears.

This antidote, also include a diagram that conveys how taking action works toward curing our fears.

Action 1: It is critical to know, that action cures fear. As such, find a way to isolate your fears. Once you do this, you can then begin to take constructive action to face those fears. Taking action on the thing you fear most is highly effective. If you don't take action, your fears will grow.

Action 2: Project (or force) your confidence. Here are some ways to do this:

> **a.** Force yourself to sit in the front row of your training classes, sit nearest the boss in meetings, put yourself out there, etc.

> **b.** Speak up. Participate. Engage.

c. Make sure you make and keep eye contact with everyone with whom you speak. Force yourself to not instantly look away. Establish your presence.

d. When you walk, walk with purpose. Consider walking 25% faster.

e. Smile big and act as if you were confident. Fake it till you make it.

f. Stand tall, and act like a person with pride. People respond more positively to such a presence, which will up your confidence.

Action 3: Take time to actively envision yourself successfully executing that thing which you fear. Many times, our fears are tied up in our perception that we can't or won't be able to do something well. A simple action that we can take to calm our nerves about a fear of our inability to do something is to imagine, over and over again, our doing that thing well, or perfectly. Doing so will not only ensure you do that thing better, but you will have less angst leading up to the doing of that thing.

Action 4: Take massive action to only allow positive thoughts in your mind. Watching or reading the news, allowing ourselves to think negatively, being around gossipers, or participating in gossiping, will detract from your confidence, and thus incubate your fears.

Action 5: Practice following what your conscience tells you is right. In other words, listen to your gut. By doing so, you will prevent a toxic guilt complex. Trust your gut. If something feels wrong, it probably is, so don't do it.

Action 6: Release your fear of other people, and of their judgements. Remember that other people are just as human as you and I. Also keep in mind, that people more often than not, really mean well. And deep down inside, they are actually nice, and don't have the negative judgements of us that we typically conjure up in our minds.

Be sure to review the 'Take Action Diagram' on the following pages, as it will help illuminate why taking action on your fears is helpful.

Once you have reviewed the diagram, consider coming back to the actions mentioned earlier, and pick any item, and **decide** to **take action** on it today.

TAKE ACTION DIAGRAM

We are fearful of those things that are outside our comfort zone. The unknown has always brought discomfort to even the greatest of us. This model objectively demonstrates how when we take actions/risks towards facing our fears, we eventually make progress towards overcoming those fears. [4]

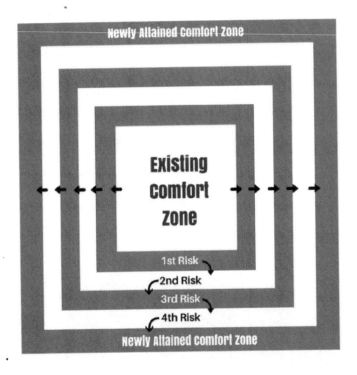

Imagine yourself standing within the center of the model, which is your existing comfort zone. As you take incremental risks, you move outward on this model, to higher level risks, acquiring new levels of confidence in the process. This level of confidence then allows for you to keep moving (outward) towards that main fear, until you've faced it. At this point, the discomfort of doing that fearful event again should be much less severe, as you have graduated into your newly attained comfort zone.

This model also demonstrates why even after we've accomplished a fear inducing goal, why we may continue to still have fears. It's important to note, that in most cases, the fear we are experiencing won't be the same fear as before. As we choose to stretch ourselves to accomplish bigger or more challenging goals, new fears will arise due to the uncertainty of accomplishing those goals.

To track the progress of the actions you seek to take over time, (over the next 66 days), there are weekly diagrams that have been included for use in **Appendix A.

ANTIDOTE 4: THE SELF-CONFIDENCE FORMULA

The following Self-Confidence Formula was derived from Napoleon Hill's classic book, 'Think and Grow Rich'.[5] I have included it because I use it myself, and because of the powerful effect it has had on my life.

I have found that it has the most optimal effect when it is read consistently, in its entirety, and aloud with deliberate energy every morning just after waking up.

By reading this mantra daily as a ritual, noticeable changes to your confidence levels may be experienced. As such, you will be positioning yourself to approach your fears with the heightened courage needed to conquer them. **Here it is:**

1. I know that I have the ability to achieve the object of my Definite Purpose in life. Therefore, I demand of myself persistent, continuous action towards its attainment, and I here and now promise to take such action.

2. I realize the dominating thoughts of my mind will eventually reproduce themselves in outward, physical action and gradually transform themselves into physical reality. Therefore, I will concentrate my thoughts for 30 minutes daily upon the task of thinking of the person I intend to become, thereby creating in my mind a clear mental picture of that person.

3. I know through the principle of <u>autosuggestion</u> that any desire I persistently hold in my mind will eventually seek expression through some practical means of attaining the object. Therefore, I will devote 10 minutes daily to demanding of myself the development of self-confidence.

4. I have clearly written down a description of my Definite Chief Aim in life. I will never stop trying until I have developed sufficient self-confidence for its attainment.

5. I fully realize that no wealth or position can long endure unless built upon truth and justice. Therefore, I will engage in no transaction that does not benefit all whom it affects. I will succeed by attracting to myself the forces I wish to use, and the cooperation of other people. I will induce others to serve me because of my willingness to serve others. I will eliminate hatred, envy, jealousy, selfishness and cynicism by developing love for all humanity because I know that a negative attitude towards others can never bring me success. I will cause others to believe in me, because I will believe in them, and in myself. I will sign my name to this formula, commit it to memory and repeat it aloud once a day, with full faith that it will gradually influence my thoughts and actions so that I will become a self-reliant and successful person.

MINDSET MANTRA: As part of antidote 4 I've also included the following mantra, which was written by Walter D. Wintle.[6]

This mantra is a great reminder of the power thought has on our life outcomes. I've included it because it has been a helpful reminder for me on the power belief and mindset can have on how we show up in life.

I believe, with constant review, it can strengthen your belief in your ability to *will* change, and to use your *mind* to defeat the challenges that lay before you.

(See the next page to review the mindset mantra.)

MINDSET MANTRA

If you *think* you are beaten, you are,

If you *think* you dare not, you don't

If you like to win, but you *think* you can't,

It's almost certain you won't.

If you *think* you'll lose, you're lost

For out of the world we find,

Success begins with a person's *will* –

It's all in the state of *mind*.

If you *think* you are outclassed, you are,

You've got to *think* high to rise.

You've got to be sure of yourself before

You can ever win a prize.

Life's battles don't always go

To the stronger or faster human

But soon or late the one who wins

Is the one WHO *THINKS* HE CAN!

ANTIDOTE 5: EFFECTIVE FEAR CONQUERING AFFIRMATIONS

If you are not familiar with affirmations, they are essentially statements said to oneself, with conviction about a perceived truth. They are a way of programming one's mind into believing what you are telling it.

Affirmations can be useful for strengthening our minds against a number of self-limiting beliefs. And they are especially affective for helping people manage a lack of confidence or a strong sense of fear towards doing something.

If you want to learn more about what affirmations are, and how to make them work for you, I highly recommend you read the Psychology Today article, by Ronald Alexander Ph.D. titled: '5 Steps to Make Affirmations Work for You'. [7]

(See selected bibliography at the end of the book to learn more about where you can find this article on the web.)

The following phrases are the most powerful Fear Conquering affirmations I've used. They are most impactful when read daily, out loud to yourself. It is especially effective if you look into a mirror, directly into your eyes, when reciting these affirmations (mirror technique not 100% necessary, especially if you are driving, etc.).

For the sixth one, fill in the blank with whichever title you are having doubts about, or fills you with fear due to self-perceived feelings of inadequacies. For example; if you have a fear that you aren't a strong leader, recite the following: I am a strong leader. Similarly, if you fear you are not good public speaker, you can recite the following: I am a great public speaker. Also, if you fear you are not a good conversationalist, just recite the following: I am a great conversationalist, and so on and so forth.

You can also easily interchange the adjective of **Great** on this sixth affirmation with whichever one you wish to be more of, i.e. good, powerful, successful, calm, peaceful, happy, etc.

- **I AM FEARLESS.**
- **WHATEVER HAPPENS TO ME, I CAN HANDLE IT.**
- **I EXUDE CONFIDENCE.**
- **I AM POWERFUL, POSITIVE, AND ENERGETIC.**
- **I LOVE MYSELF, AS WELL AS OTHERS.**
- **I AM A GREAT_____.**

On the following pages, I've included a diagram that can help you track how affirmations are impacting your feelings of empowerment over time.

The exercise is optional, but can help you observe and track progress.

PAIN TO EMPOWERMENT CONTINUUM

DIAGRAM: I learned of this diagram from Susan Jeffers, Ph.D., after reading her book, 'Feel the Fear and Do it Anyway'.[8] It has served as a very useful way to track my progress on my feelings of confidence.

With knowledge that you can track how you feel about yourself, and how you perceive yourself in terms of handling your fears, you can gradually improve your situation. That which gets measured, can improve. As such, this diagram is an excellent way to track your progress towards becoming more empowered via the affirmations antidote, (or can be used to track your feelings of progress for the entire formula), towards becoming fearless. How you measure yourself is purely subjective and relative to your situation, but then again, so is fear.

An important thing to keep in mind, is that the secret to handling our fears, is our ability to move ourselves from a place of pain (see left side of diagram), to a place of feeling empowered (see right side of diagram). When we are in a place of pain, we feel helpless, we feel depressed, have a feeling of paralysis (Can't, Won't, or Don't want to do Anything), and are generally apathetic.

However, when we are empowered, we feel we are capable of making decisions. We have more energy, we take more action, and we conduct ourselves from a place of passion. Observe the diagram below.

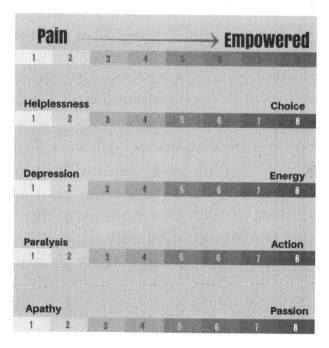

**To track the impact the affirmations are having on you (over the next 66 days), this diagram has been included in Appendix B.

ANTIDOTE 6: AFFIRMATIONS ON STEROIDS - HYPNOSIS

One of the most effective fear busting practices I've used has been of a hypnotic nature. If hypnosis seems foreign to you, or taboo, I highly recommend you do a google search on the science of it.

But if the idea of it makes you uncomfortable, then just skip this section.

However, if you plan to skip this section, know this: There are many misconceptions about the practice due to a lack of knowledge on the subject. For me, hypnosis is very similar to an affirmation, the primary difference is I am allowing someone else's voice to drown out my self-limiting beliefs, vs. using my own with an affirmation.

It's just another form of programming our mind with the thoughts we want. If you read up on hypnosis, but you are still uncomfortable with the thought of it, feel free to ignore this section.

With that being said, this method is a great addition to your toolbox of ways to face your anxieties, fears, and lack of confidence. Before I give you the list, here is a brief example of my initial experience with Hypnosis.

The first time I used hypnosis, it was during the 2nd day of a week-long professional conference I was attending early in my professional career. The conference was packed with engineers, analysts, and technicians involved in digital geospatial-aviation solutions (a fancy way of saying, smart maps ala Zillow, but for airports.)

At the time I was very uncomfortable in my role. I was working for a boutique engineering firm, getting paid very well for my age. However, I secretly despised what I was doing. Deep down inside, I knew I was meant to do so much more. As such, every time I found myself sitting at a table with other engineers and the like, I would start to feel extremely insecure. I felt like I was a fraud, although well educated in my field, and having strong relevant professional experiences to rely on.

The conference was to last a few days, and I remember after that first day at the conference, feeling so uncomfortable, that when I got back to my house, I sat down and did some research on my computer, on how I could feel more comfortable in those particular types of situations. What I came across, and eventually used, was a downloadable hypnosis session. I downloaded the program that night, and listened to it the very next morning, right before heading out to the conference. I didn't feel any different after the download at first, so just shrugged it off and went to my conference, prepared to push through another uncomfortable day.

However; something seemingly miraculous happened. When the conference's lunch break began, I went outside, and sat at an empty table to eat. Before I knew it, an analyst and his boss, asked if they could sit down at the table. I said yes. After that, two engineers sat down. Two minutes later, a group of three friends from the aviation industry also sat down. Before I knew it, the table was full. The miraculous thing that occurred, was that the moment I realized the table was full, I almost immediately experienced a warm peaceful-like feeling overcome me. It was a very noticeable feeling.

During that lunch break, I had zero feelings of discomfort. In fact, I was actually enjoying the conversations that I was having with my new professional acquaintances. It was at that moment, at that conference, that I realized the power of hypnosis.

One thing to keep in mind, is that hypnosis isn't a cure all. It is merely another set of tools that you can use to weaken the resistance you have towards facing your fears so, you can express your bold ideas and live more courageously.

Here are six very powerful hypnosis downloads I used to help me overcome some of my most pressing fears. You'll notice, not all of them directly reference the term fear, i.e. the first three. However, I've listed these particular sessions, because in my experience, a lack of belief, love, and trust in ourselves can be our biggest roadblocks, as we seek to do those things which cause us the most fear. In a sense, they are the foundation of becoming fearless.

Without further ado, here is the list:

Download 1: <u>Believe in Yourself</u>

Download 2: <u>Love Yourself</u>

Download 3: <u>Trust Yourself</u>

Download 4: <u>Confidence Injection</u>

Download 5: <u>Overcome Your Fears</u>

Download 6: <u>Fearless Public Speaker</u>

To gain access to these downloads, go to
uncommonknowledge.com and search for each
download term I listed above.

Lastly, and for your own awareness, there are other
hypnosis programs out there, but I've appreciated
the quality downloads that are produced by a
company named **Uncommon Knowledge LTD**.
If these six recommendations don't meet your
needs, you can simply go to
uncommonknowledge.com and browse through
their immense library. Or do a search on the web
for different programs.

ANTIDOTE 7: TWENTY POWER QUOTES FOR CONQUERING FEAR

Below you will find 20 power quotes that you can reference at your leisure. Once you have read all of them, consider coming back to the ones that really speak to you.

The quote that moves you the most is the quote that will be most helpful to read when you need to take action on anything that you are resistant to do.

Quote 1: "Fear, the worst of all enemies, can be effectively cured by forced repetition of acts of courage." - **Napoleon Hill**

Quote 2: "Fearlessness isn't a divine gift. Fearlessness is a daily practice." - **Robin Sharma**

Quote 3: "There is only one thing that makes a dream impossible to achieve: the fear of failure." - **Paulo Coelho**

Quote 4: "Too many of us are not living our dreams because we are living our fears." - **Les Brown**

Quote 5: "There is only one way to avoid criticism: Do nothing, say nothing, and be nothing." - **Aristotle**

Quote 6: "A human becomes fearless by accepting his/her fears. It is not a question of bravery. It is simply seeing into the facts of life and realizing that these fears are natural." - **Osho**

Quote 7: "He who is not every day conquering some fear has not learned the secret of life." - **Ralph Waldo Emerson**

Quote 8: "Safe is Risky" - **Seth Godin**

Quote 9:   "Life is being on the wire, everything else is just waiting" - **Karl Wallenda**

Quote 10:   "Only those who dare to fail greatly can ever achieve greatly " - **Robert F. Kennedy**

Quote 11:   "Only those who risk going too far can possibly find out how far they can go." - **T.S. Eliot**

Quote 12:   "Greatness lives on the edge of destruction" - **Will Smith**

Quote 13:   "Life shrinks or expands in proportion to one's courage" - **Anais Nin**

Quote 14:   "Do not wait to strike till the iron is hot: but make it hot by striking" - **William B. Sprague**

Quote 15: "It is never too late to be what you might have been" - **George Elliot**

Quote 16: "The most important thing to remember is this: To be ready at any moment to give up what you are for what you might become. " - **D.E.B Dubois**

Quote 17: "Twenty years from now you will be more disappointed by the things you didn't do than by the ones you did do. So throw off the bowlines. Sail from the safe harbor. Catch the trade winds in your sails. Explore. Dream. Discover." - **Mark Twain**

Quote 18: "The only person who never makes mistakes is the person who never does anything" - **Dennis Waitely**

Quote 19: "People who don't take risks generally make about two big mistakes a year. People who do take risks generally make about two big mistakes a year." - **Peter Drucker**

Quote 20: "It is only by risking our persons from one hour to another that we live at all" - **William James**

ANTIDOTE 8: POWER QUESTIONS FOR BANISHING FEAR

The following four questions will bring a new level of clarity to every situation where fear may be involved. It is suggested that you honestly ask these questions of yourself.

Similarly, when faced with a future challenge or situation which induces fear in you, ask yourselves these questions, and wait for your inside voice to answer the question for you. You should find that these questions have a calming effect on you, gently banishing the fears that your mind has potentially built up around the task at hand.

Question 1: What is really on the other side of this thing I am fearing at the moment?

The answer is always... NOTHING.

Question 2: If I knew that I could handle anything that came my way, what would I possibly have to fear?

The answers is... NOTHING.

Question 3: If the worst possible outcome related to doing this thing that is making me so afraid, actually happened, would I be able to handle the outcome?

The answer is...YES.

Question 4: If I let this fear get the best of me, and allow it to keep me from doing that which am afraid to accomplish, will I, on my deathbed, regret that I had not made the decision to do that thing which I so feared?

The answer is... **IT IS UP TO YOU**.

ANTIDOTE 9: FEAR BUSTING TED TALK VIDEOS

To help put a stop to fear and its shrewd ability to limit our lives, I've curated four powerful Ted Talks. My hope is that you'll watch them and learn some new tactics that you can use to build your confidence and overcome your fears.

Below each image is a brief synopsis of each video. You can read the synopsis to get an idea of what the video is about before you commit to watching the whole thing. When you are ready to watch the video, just click its associated image or the provided link.

(See next page for 1st video)

VIDEO 1: AMY CUDDY

This is an extremely inspirational video by Social Psychologist **Amy Cuddy**. She provides amazing insight into how research is starting to suggest that we are influenced by our own non-verbal communication to ourselves. In short, she reveals how our non-verbal's (like body language) can influence how we think and feel about ourselves. It's great information to help you build confidence so you can become fearless. Her last suggestion is what is most important. "Fake it till you Become it".

TO SEE VIDEO GO HERE:

https://www.ted.com/talks/amy_cuddy_your_body_language_shapes_who_you_are

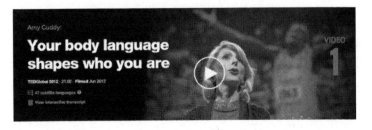

VIDEO 2: TIM FERRISS

Author of 'Tools of Titans' and productivity guru Tim Ferris gives a nice intellectual breakdown on how he learned to deconstruct his fears so he can eventually conquer them. If you watch the video till the end, he eventually ties all of his examples together to help you understand how you can overcome fear. His last two messages are by far the most important. "Fear is your friend." and "What is the worst that could happen?"

TO SEE VIDEO GO HERE:

https://www.ted.com/talks/tim_ferriss_smash_fear_learn_anything

VIDEO 3: JOE KOWAN

An entertaining and uplifting video that details how singer-songwriter Joe Kowan eventually learned how to overcome his fear of being on stage. Joe does this by ritually singing a stage fright song that he created before every event he does. It's very powerful and is a must watch for those who need to build confidence for getting on stage or in front of large groups of people. Click on the image above to watch.

TO SEE VIDEO GO HERE:

https://www.ted.com/talks/joe_kowan_how_i_beat_stage_fright

VIDEO 4: JIA JANG

Author of 'Rejection Proof', Jia Jiang, provides a very funny, informative, and helpful video for overcoming our fears. He starts slow, but his message really picks up steam half way through. By the end of the video, you will have laughed a dozen times and you will most certainly have gained some powerful insights for overcoming your fears and dealing with rejection. Jia Jiang's last statement really knocks it out of the park, when he admonishes that we embrace our fears, because it is in doing so, that we are bound to discover our biggest opportunities.

TO SEE VIDEO GO HERE:

https://www.ted.com/talks/jia_jiang_what_i_learned_from_100_days_of_rejection

ANTIDOTE 10: FOLLOW YOUR FIRE

Why are we so afraid to do what we truly want in this life? Why are we always letting other people's opinions drive the decisions we make?

Too many of us tuck our dreams and true interests away in some small corner at the first sign of disapproval from others. We don't we follow our own heart, we don't we follow our fire. Why?

I can't say I have the answer for the questions above, as they differ from person to person. All I can do is wonder with you.

For much of my life, I was guilty of succumbing to the external pressures of my contemporaries. Always buckling under the pressure to do something I didn't want to do, or becoming something I was not.

For too many years I let the outside world dictate how I should believe and live in my inside world. I let other people suggest how I should think, believe, and feel about a certain topic, approach, or career choice. I allowed my opinion of events or circumstances to be put on hold, to make way for the opinions and beliefs of others.

One day though, I realized what was happening in my life, and I didn't like it. I realized that I was allowing myself to be subjugated. I was subjugated. I was a serf, a follower, a conquered person.

Robert Greene, said it so well in his book 'Mastery', as he pinpointed exactly what was happening to me all those years ago. In fact, it is what happens to all of us when we don't follow our inclinations. An excerpt from his book states the following:

"Conforming to social norms, you will listen more to others than to your own voice. You may choose a career path based on what peers and parents tell you, or on what seems lucrative. If you lose contact with (your) inner calling, you can have some success in life, but eventually your lack of true desire catches up with you. Your work becomes mechanical. You come to live for leisure and immediate pleasures."[13]

Fortunately, a day came when I said enough was enough. Like the statement I made above, I was tired of always feeling guilty. I was fed up with feeling frustrated, empty, fearful, uncertain, and uninspired. Not to mention, exhausted from carrying around the weight of responsibility that was forced upon me by someone else's philosophy.

Robert Greene also posited "You may grow frustrated and depressed, never realizing that the source of it is your alienation from your own creative potential." Which is exactly what was occurring.

Fortunately, it was such a realization that allowed for me put my foot down. I was lucky enough to notice over a series of random moments, how diminished my internal drive was. My fire and zest for life was at an all-time low. In realizing that my internal flame had come to a flicker, I knew that something was not right. I knew that I had abandoned my pursuit of expressing my creative potential.

As such, I decided to change. I decided to ignore the noise coming from the mouths of others. I decided to listen to what I really wanted, and to follow through on those desires. I made up my mind to follow my inclinations, my interests, my fire.

By no means was this an easy thing to do. In fact, it took all of the resources mentioned throughout this book to prep me to the point where I was confident enough to get off my knees, rise, and stand tall against the uncertainty of the world. It took some time, effort, and a final bold decision to pursue my fire. But I did it, and so can you.

So, if you are afraid to do what you truly want in this life, don't be. You only have one life to live, and none of us are getting out of here alive anyway.

If you are always letting other people's opinions drive the decisions you make, respectfully, stop! Your opinions matter, **what interests you is important**.

No more tucking your dreams and true interests away, no more hiding your talents because others disapprove of them. Please, follow your own heart, follow your inclinations to express your own creative potential. Please, follow your fire!

Following your fire is the final antidote of the fearless formula. It is the last act, because it requires the most self-examination and courage to act on your insights; however, it also harnesses the most potential to help you live confidently, boldly, fearlessly.

To help you follow you fire, you first need to know exactly what **your fire** is. As such, this antidote consists of an exercise to help you discover what your calling is, so you can follow it.

Once you've completed the self-discovery aspect of this antidote, your job is to focus on bringing it to life by making plans to live it.

FIND YOUR FIRE EXERCISE

1. Are you satisfied with the quality of your life? If not why not? If yes, elaborate?

2. Is your occupation personally fulfilling? What would make it more fulfilling?

3. What do you consider to be your greatest strengths? Make a list.

4. What do you consider are your biggest weaknesses? Make a list.

5. What do other people tell you are your greatest strengths and weaknesses? If no one has ever told you, reach out to your closest friend/family member and ask them. Make a list.

6. If you had only one year to live, what would you choose as your occupation(s)?

7. If you had only one year to live, what physical or mental characteristics would you improve?

8. If you had only one year to live what contribution would you want to make to society?

9. If you had only one year to live what spiritual commitment would you make?

10. What recreational activities would you undertake if you only had one year to live?

11. If you had 7 years to live, would your answers be any different? If so, how?

12. Now, if you had actually passed away, what would you want your obituary to read?

13. What has been the most blissful moment of your life so far?

14. Can you relive this happy moment again in a similar or another way? How?

15. What are your major fears? How can you develop the confidence to overcome them?

16. In what way do you exhibit the faith and courage to overcome diversity? Can you improve in this area? How?

17. What financial goal would you accomplish?

18. Do you allow the negative thinking of others to interfere with your progress?

19. When you daydream, what do you see?

20. What occupations or vocations do you find yourself dreaming of?

21. Do you have any talents that you don't regularly use? Why aren't you using them? How could you use them?

22. What is the single most important goal you would like to achieve before you die? If this is so important, why don't you have it now?

23. What are you naturally curious about? What subjects to you enjoy getting lost in?

24. When you go to the bookstore, what section to you gravitate towards, even when you aren't going to buy a book?

25. What do you enjoy helping people with?

26. When was the last time you lost track of time because you were enjoying what you were doing so much?

27. If you didn't care what anyone thought, what would you do?

28. If your duty was the sincere and honest development of your true potential, what steps would you take to develop that potential?

29. What would the ideal physical, financial, mental, and spiritual form of you look like if you could make it so with one wish?

30. If you had 100% certainty that you wouldn't fail, what would you start today?

CONCLUSION AND IMPLEMENTATION

By answering all of the questions carefully, and giving each one sincere and thorough consideration, you should now have a much deeper awareness of who you are, what makes you happy, and what you should be doing with your life.

Study your answers carefully, and fill in the space below as articulately and thoroughly as possible.

MY CALLING, MY FIRE IS:

_____

_____

_____

When every decision you make, every action you take is aligned with the fulfillment of the life objective you've just listed above, you will begin to truly live fearlessly.

BONUS: 10 CONFIDENCE HACKS

The purpose of this last bonus section is to give you one last set of tools to help you fortify your confidence levels.

The more confidence tools you have in your toolbox, the better your odds will be for crushing your fears. These confidence hacks are some of the most effective methods for building confidence.

1. EXERCISE

This one is simple. Go exercise! Staying in shape improves your confidence in multiple ways. The first way, is that it makes you feel better on a physiological level.

Exercise will help you manage your weight better, it will help you reduce feelings of anxiety and depression, give you increased levels of energy, while improving overall feelings of well-being.

In addition to this, when you exercise, you inevitably look good. When you look good, it's a lot easier to be happy with yourself. When you look in the mirror and like what you see, you subtly strengthen your confidence in yourself. If you want to know how to build confidence, build your physique. It's like the saying goes... "when you look good, you play good".

2. SET GOALS FOR YOURSELF

This may sound counter-intuitive, but setting goals for yourself before you have the confidence to achieve them can help you become more confident.

Marci G. Fox, Ph.D., outlines exactly how in her collaborative book 'Think Confident Be Confident' .

I can attest to this from my own experience as well. Every time I gave myself a big goal to aim for, I inevitably began acting with more purpose and conviction, so as to make that goal a reality.

When you set a goal for yourself, you unconsciously affirm to yourself, that you believe you have what it takes to reach that goal. And every time you take action on those goals, you reinforce that confidence in yourself.

3. PRACTICE SOLITUDE

Taking some time to be alone with your thoughts can improve your self-esteem. One might initially think that being alone would create feelings of loneliness, but this is untrue. If it were true, then it wouldn't be very good for improving confidence.

However; solitude is the exact opposite of being lonely. In essences, solitude is the art of being alone, without feeling lonely.

Being able to spend time with yourself, alone, allows for you to drown out the voices from outside. By doing this, you can get to listen to your own thoughts.

Being alone to listen to, consider, and respond to your own thoughts without external interruptions, will strengthen your self-awareness. And having a stronger sense of self will lead to higher levels of self-esteem.

4. PRACTICE GRATITUDE

When we practice expressing gratitude, we boost our self-worth and self-esteem. When we become aware of how much we actually have, or how much we've accomplished in our lives, we give ourselves a small confidence injection. To back this claim, the Journal of Applied Sport Psychology conducted a 2014 study, and discovered a link between practiced gratitude and high self-esteem.

Practicing gratitude also helps reduce a handful of other toxic feelings like resentment, frustration, and depression. This in turn leads to an improved overall sense of well-being, which supports heightened levels of confidence. Time to start practicing an attitude of gratitude.

5. TAKE A COLD SHOWER

Taking cold showers works like a charm for two reasons; one is scientific, and the other is psychological.
The scientific aspect as to why cold showers can help build your self-confidence is due to the anti-depressive effect that stems from activating our sympathetic nervous system and increasing the blood level of beta-endorphin and norepinephrine.

What this essentially means, is that cold showers are good at flooding the mood-regulating areas of our brains with happy neurotransmitters and mood-boosting endorphins. It's basically like getting a runner's high.

The psychological aspect is related to the will-power that must be exhibited to get yourself to actually do the deed. Taking a cold-shower is very uncomfortable, requiring a strong force of will to get in and stay in for the entire duration of the shower.

Doing this time and time again strengthens your determination, and will give you the sense that you have conquered a weaker part of yourself. All in all, taking cold showers is a sure-fire way to boost your confidence and make yourself feel like a champion.

6. POWER POSE

Amy Cuddy, in her Ted Talk Video (see antidote 9), posits the scientific benefits of power posing to increasing self-confidence. She does a good job of providing research-backed insights that suggest we can influence ourselves with our own non-verbal communication.

If we make ourselves stand or pose in a powerful way, we can impact how confident we feel about ourselves.

As an added way to build confidence, be sure you are paying attention to the message your own body language is sending. Don't hesitate to strike a pose from time to time.

7. MEDITATE

Mediation is the practice of quieting your mind and disciplining your attention. When done correctly, it can help put your mind at ease and silence your hyperactive thoughts.

Similar to the benefits of solitude, when you practice meditating you increase your awareness of just about everything, including your strengths and limitations. And when you gain a better sense of self-awareness, you simultaneously gain confidence.

8. TRY SOMETHING NEW

When we try something new, we open ourselves up for creating new experiences and seeing the world in a different way. Sometimes, all it takes to give our confidence a boost is a slight change in our perspectives.

When we put ourselves out there to do something outside of our normal routines, we give ourselves the opportunity to be energized by new people and unique experiences.

The small step of taking some form of action to try something new can have immediate benefits to your confidence as well. Be sure to get out there and do something, anything, just make sure it's new.

9. FORCED SPONTANEITY

Many of us operate our daily lives following a routine script we've set up for ourselves. We do most of our daily undertakings in a mechanical way because it feels safe, familiar, and because we think we know what the outcome of our standard activities are going to be.
It's okay to have a routine; however, mixing it up a bit, is exactly what you may need to ignite your confidence.

When we force ourselves to be spontaneous, we stretch ourselves. We allow ourselves to be open to potential discomfort, and the uncertainty of the unknown.

Being spontaneous exposes us to situations that we don't have an easy script to rely on to get us through the experience comfortably. As such, spontaneity will force you to adapt.

After being spontaneous a few times, you will come to trust that you can handle almost any situation, regardless of whether or not you were prepared for it.

10. PUSH YOUR LIMITS

This is my last suggestion, and it is by far my favorite. I like it because anyone can apply it, and it will produce positive results in multiple areas of your life.
My last suggestion for building confidence is this: If you push your limits and make great efforts towards any endeavor in your life, you will set yourself for a flood of confidence.

Here's why. When you push yourself to go the extra mile, to do more than what others expect of you, when do more than you even think you should do, you create an opportunity to stand out in a positive way to others.

You're boss or colleagues will be impressed with your effort, and their praise will inject you with confidence.

In addition, when you push your limits you will come to realize that you are capable of so much more than you initially thought yourself to be. Coming to this realization will ignite your confidence to new, potentially staggering heights.

ONE LAST THING ON CONFIDENCE

The results we get in life will be in direct proportion to the quantity and quality of the risks we take. And the grandness of those risks we took, will we be dictated by the confidence we had when making them. Since you now know how to build confidence, you are in a better position to win in life.
When you practice these 10 confidence hacks routinely, alongside the 10 antidotes, you will be better positioned to crush your future victories with ease.

On top of that, you will be equipping yourself to win the internal battles over fear and adversity with authority and finesse. Follow these tips on how to build confidence, so you can start crushing life.

FINAL WORDS

A FINAL WORD OF CAUTION:

There is nothing more crushing in your pursuit of becoming your absolute best or in deciding to become who you truly want to be, then by having someone within your inner circle doubt your intentions and doubt your possibilities.

"THERE IS NOTHIN ENLIGHTENED ABOUT SHRINKING SO THAT OTHER PEOPLE WILL NOT FEEL INSECURE AROUND YOU. WE ARE ALL MEANT TO SHINE."

- MARIANNE WILLIAMSON -

As you've probably experienced, fear and doubt can spread swiftly like a virus. As such, you must take proper precautions to make yourself immune to its infection.

A good starting point, in making yourself immune, is to understand that doubters are simply afraid. They are afraid of not living up to their potential, afraid that you may outshine them. These individuals, will <u>claw</u> and scrape, and try to hurt you, to keep you fearful of life, **fearful of your very best**, and they do this because they have yet to find the courage to face their fears and pursue their potential.

If possible, remove the doubters from your life. Remove, as best as you can, anyone who doubts your potential, who doubts your skills, your abilities, your choices, your greatness. If you can't completely remove these people from your life, then distance yourself from them. Spend as little time around them as possible, so as to minimize their negative influences on you.

If distancing yourself from them is not an option, then you must create a mental firewall to negate their negativity, to negate their doubts. A simple way to do this, is to convince yourself that their judgement no longer holds the weight that it once had. Seeing yourself as a lion, and 'them' as the sheep, and then remembering the following quote will start the strengthening of your mental firewall.

"A LION DOESN'T CONCERN HIMSELF WITH THE OPINIONS OF THE SHEEP."

- ANONYMOUS -

A FINAL WORD OF ENCOURAGEMENT:

Congratulations, you now have the means to create your own fearless formula. The choice to go fearless is now solely up to you.

I encourage you to decide to be confident today, to make the decision to believe that you can handle whatever this world throws at you. If you make this simple decision, and practice this formula, you are in effect deciding to be fearless, and as a result, you will be.

If your fears begin to creep back in, remember that you can rely on the power of belief and the power of pursuit, to drive your fears away.

As you move forward towards becoming fearless, towards taking on new and greater challenges, I am confident everything in life will change for you. Believe that you can do whatever it is that you want to do. Have faith in yourself, have faith in your vision, believe that you deserve the best, because my friend, you do. Go Fearless!

With great respect,

NATE LEE MORALES

APPENDIX A: ACTION EXERCISES

Use this exercise to track yourself taking one risk per week, towards a **specific** fear. If you do so for the next 66 days, you will create a habit of facing your fears. Fill in the top section of the column on the right **(Risk or Actions Towards Fear Of:)** with the specific fear you are trying to overcome.

In the following boxes below, you will enter in the one specific risk you take each week to move you forward towards conquering the fear you outlined on the top section.

This image below is just a sample

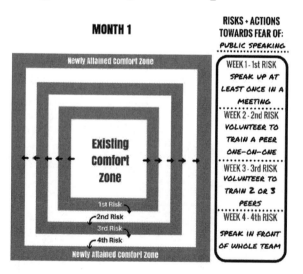

Use the action exercises on the next few pages as part of your workbook.

APPENDIX A:

Below is **month 1**, with 4 specific action/risks for you to take towards a precise fear you have.

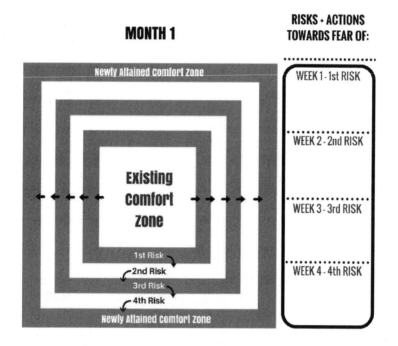

APPENDIX A:

Below is **month 2**, with 4 specific action/risks for you to take towards a precise fear you have.

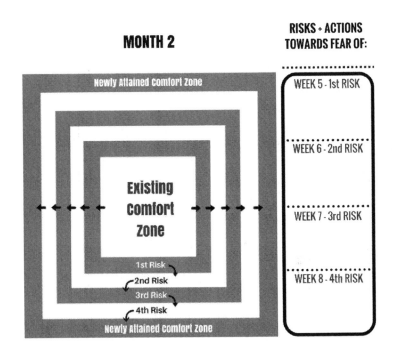

APPENDIX A:

Below is **month 3**, with 4 specific action/risks for you to take towards a precise fear you have.

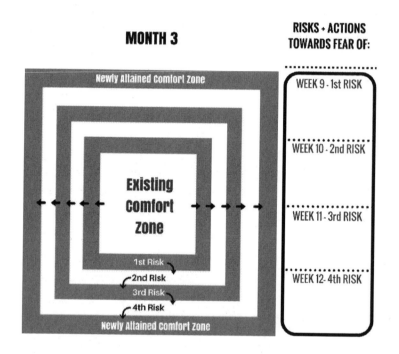

APPENDIX B: EMPOWERMENT TRACKING EXERCISES

Take inventory of your progress towards becoming fearless for the next 66 days, using the 'pain to empower' diagram from antidote 5. To use it, simply add a check mark along the spectrum, pinpointing how you feel your empowerment levels rank on a scale from 1 – 8 at the end of every week (1 being the worst, and nearest to pain, and 8 being the best and nearest to feelings of empowerment). Tracking like this can help to provide a sense of accomplishment, which can help you push through the entire duration of the formula.

Quantify Results to Make Measurable Progress: Wherever you place your check mark on each of the four spectrums, you can use the location (1 -8) of that check mark as the number to enter in the boxes below. By doing this, you put a number to your progress. In fact, at the end of each week, you can tally up your score for each spectrum (divide it by 4) and then enter it into the **TOTAL SCORE box** at the bottom. By quantifying your improvement, you can make measurable progress over time. For instance, the hypothetical total score on the next page is the total of each spectrum score, divided by 4. i.e. 7+4+6+8 = 25   so then 25 ÷ 4 equals **6.25** (See example on next page).

APPENDIX B:

EXAMPLE

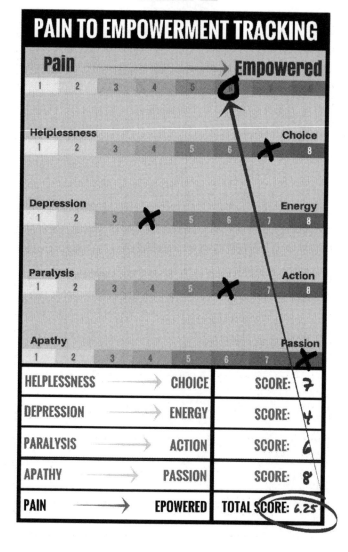

PAIN TO EMPOWERMENT TRACKING

Pain ⟶ Empowered

HELPLESSNESS ⟶ CHOICE	SCORE:	7
DEPRESSION ⟶ ENERGY	SCORE:	4
PARALYSIS ⟶ ACTION	SCORE:	6
APATHY ⟶ PASSION	SCORE:	8
PAIN ⟶ EPOWERED	TOTAL SCORE:	6.25

APPENDIX B:

WEEK 1

PAIN TO EMPOWERMENT TRACKING

Pain ⟶ **Empowered**

| 1 | 2 | 3 | 4 | 5 | 6 | 7 | |

Helplessness **Choice**

| 1 | 2 | 3 | 4 | 5 | 6 | 7 | 8 |

Depression **Energy**

| 1 | 2 | 3 | 4 | 5 | 6 | 7 | 8 |

Paralysis **Action**

| 1 | 2 | 3 | 4 | 5 | 6 | 7 | 8 |

Apathy **Passion**

| 1 | 2 | 3 | 4 | 5 | 6 | 7 | 8 |

HELPLESSNESS ⟶ CHOICE		SCORE:
DEPRESSION ⟶ ENERGY		SCORE:
PARALYSIS ⟶ ACTION		SCORE:
APATHY ⟶ PASSION		SCORE:
PAIN ⟶ EPOWERED		TOTAL SCORE:

APPENDIX B:

WEEK 2

PAIN TO EMPOWERMENT TRACKING

Pain						→ Empowered	
1	2	3	4	5	6	7	8

Helplessness							Choice
1	2	3	4	5	6	7	8

Depression							Energy
1	2	3	4	5	6	7	8

Paralysis							Action
1	2	3	4	5	6	7	8

Apathy							Passion
1	2	3	4	5	6	7	8

HELPLESSNESS → CHOICE	SCORE:
DEPRESSION → ENERGY	SCORE:
PARALYSIS → ACTION	SCORE:
APATHY → PASSION	SCORE:
PAIN → EPOWERED	TOTAL SCORE:

APPENDIX B:

WEEK 3

PAIN TO EMPOWERMENT TRACKING

Pain ⟶ **Empowered**

| 1 | 2 | 3 | 4 | 5 | 6 | 7 | |

Helplessness **Choice**

| 1 | 2 | 3 | 4 | 5 | 6 | 7 | 8 |

Depression **Energy**

| 1 | 2 | 3 | 4 | 5 | 6 | 7 | 8 |

Paralysis **Action**

| 1 | 2 | 3 | 4 | 5 | 6 | 7 | 8 |

Apathy **Passion**

| 1 | 2 | 3 | 4 | 5 | 6 | 7 | 8 |

HELPLESSNESS ⟶ CHOICE	SCORE:
DEPRESSION ⟶ ENERGY	SCORE:
PARALYSIS ⟶ ACTION	SCORE:
APATHY ⟶ PASSION	SCORE:
PAIN ⟶ EPOWERED	TOTAL SCORE:

APPENDIX B:

WEEK 4

PAIN TO EMPOWERMENT TRACKING

Pain						Empowered	
1	2	3	4	5	6	7	8

Helplessness						Choice	
1	2	3	4	5	6	7	8

Depression						Energy	
1	2	3	4	5	6	7	8

Paralysis						Action	
1	2	3	4	5	6	7	8

Apathy						Passion	
1	2	3	4	5	6	7	8

HELPLESSNESS ⟶ CHOICE	SCORE:
DEPRESSION ⟶ ENERGY	SCORE:
PARALYSIS ⟶ ACTION	SCORE:
APATHY ⟶ PASSION	SCORE:
PAIN ⟶ EPOWERED	TOTAL SCORE:

APPENDIX B:

WEEK 5

PAIN TO EMPOWERMENT TRACKING

Pain ⟶ **Empowered**

| 1 | 2 | 3 | 4 | 5 | 6 | 7 | 8 |

Helplessness — **Choice**

| 1 | 2 | 3 | 4 | 5 | 6 | 7 | 8 |

Depression — **Energy**

| 1 | 2 | 3 | 4 | 5 | 6 | 7 | 8 |

Paralysis — **Action**

| 1 | 2 | 3 | 4 | 5 | 6 | 7 | 8 |

Apathy — **Passion**

| 1 | 2 | 3 | 4 | 5 | 6 | 7 | 8 |

HELPLESSNESS ⟶ CHOICE		SCORE:
DEPRESSION ⟶ ENERGY		SCORE:
PARALYSIS ⟶ ACTION		SCORE:
APATHY ⟶ PASSION		SCORE:
PAIN ⟶ EPOWERED		TOTAL SCORE:

APPENDIX B:

WEEK 6

PAIN TO EMPOWERMENT TRACKING

Pain ⟶ **Empowered**

1 2 3 4 5 6 7 8

Helplessness **Choice**

1 2 3 4 5 6 7 8

Depression **Energy**

1 2 3 4 5 6 7 8

Paralysis **Action**

1 2 3 4 5 6 7 8

Apathy **Passion**

1 2 3 4 5 6 7 8

HELPLESSNESS ⟶ CHOICE	SCORE:
DEPRESSION ⟶ ENERGY	SCORE:
PARALYSIS ⟶ ACTION	SCORE:
APATHY ⟶ PASSION	SCORE:
PAIN ⟶ EPOWERED	TOTAL SCORE:

APPENDIX B:

WEEK 7

PAIN TO EMPOWERMENT TRACKING

Pain						→	Empowered
1	2	3	4	5	6	7	

Helplessness							Choice
1	2	3	4	5	6	7	8

Depression							Energy
1	2	3	4	5	6	7	8

Paralysis							Action
1	2	3	4	5	6	7	8

Apathy							Passion
1	2	3	4	5	6	7	8

HELPLESSNESS	→	CHOICE	SCORE:
DEPRESSION	→	ENERGY	SCORE:
PARALYSIS	→	ACTION	SCORE:
APATHY	→	PASSION	SCORE:
PAIN	→	EPOWERED	TOTAL SCORE:

APPENDIX B:

WEEK 8

PAIN TO EMPOWERMENT TRACKING

Pain ⟶ **Empowered**

| 1 | 2 | 3 | 4 | 5 | 6 | 7 | 8 |

Helplessness — **Choice**

| 1 | 2 | 3 | 4 | 5 | 6 | 7 | 8 |

Depression — **Energy**

| 1 | 2 | 3 | 4 | 5 | 6 | 7 | 8 |

Paralysis — **Action**

| 1 | 2 | 3 | 4 | 5 | 6 | 7 | 8 |

Apathy — **Passion**

| 1 | 2 | 3 | 4 | 5 | 6 | 7 | 8 |

HELPLESSNESS ⟶ CHOICE	SCORE:
DEPRESSION ⟶ ENERGY	SCORE:
PARALYSIS ⟶ ACTION	SCORE:
APATHY ⟶ PASSION	SCORE:
PAIN ⟶ EPOWERED	TOTAL SCORE:

APPENDIX B:

WEEK 9

PAIN TO EMPOWERMENT TRACKING

Pain ⟶ **Empowered**

| 1 | 2 | 3 | 4 | 5 | 6 | 7 | |

Helplessness — **Choice**

| 1 | 2 | 3 | 4 | 5 | 6 | 7 | 8 |

Depression — **Energy**

| 1 | 2 | 3 | 4 | 5 | 6 | 7 | 8 |

Paralysis — **Action**

| 1 | 2 | 3 | 4 | 5 | 6 | 7 | 8 |

Apathy — **Passion**

| 1 | 2 | 3 | 4 | 5 | 6 | 7 | 8 |

HELPLESSNESS ⟶ CHOICE	SCORE:
DEPRESSION ⟶ ENERGY	SCORE:
PARALYSIS ⟶ ACTION	SCORE:
APATHY ⟶ PASSION	SCORE:
PAIN ⟶ EPOWERED	TOTAL SCORE:

APPENDIX B:

WEEK 10

PAIN TO EMPOWERMENT TRACKING

Pain ⟶ **Empowered**

| 1 | 2 | 3 | 4 | 5 | 6 | 7 | 8 |

Helplessness | **Choice**

| 1 | 2 | 3 | 4 | 5 | 6 | 7 | 8 |

Depression | **Energy**

| 1 | 2 | 3 | 4 | 5 | 6 | 7 | 8 |

Paralysis | **Action**

| 1 | 2 | 3 | 4 | 5 | 6 | 7 | 8 |

Apathy | **Passion**

| 1 | 2 | 3 | 4 | 5 | 6 | 7 | 8 |

HELPLESSNESS ⟶ CHOICE	SCORE:
DEPRESSION ⟶ ENERGY	SCORE:
PARALYSIS ⟶ ACTION	SCORE:
APATHY ⟶ PASSION	SCORE:
PAIN ⟶ EPOWERED	TOTAL SCORE:

APPENDIX C: MENTAL EXERCISES

EXPERIMENT 1: VISUALIZATION Cheryl Lossie,

Ph.D., is a former lecturer of public speaking for Clemson University, and current public-speaking lecturer specializing in teaching some of the most fearless people on the planet, the U.S Special Forces, how to overcome their fears of speaking in front of people, and how to do it well. When I asked Dr. Lossie what she recommended to her students (the fearless Special Ops folks) for overcoming their fears of public speaking, she informed me that it was to simply practice visualization.

The recommendation coincided well with much of my experiences for overcoming fears, and it aligned with some of Tony Robbins suggestions on how to overcome fear as well. As such, a great mental exercise that you can conduct to help you improve your confidence in doing that thing which you fear doing, is to simply visualize.

As a best practice to visualize effectively, it is recommended, that you sit in a quiet place, with no distractions, close your eyes, and then take 2 to 5 minutes to imagine yourself executing flawlessly (in addition rebounding flawlessly, if things do go as planned) that thing which you are so afraid of doing.

- If it's public speaking, see yourself giving a flawless presentation. Also, see yourself getting that standing ovation or that positive response you are seeking from your audience once you've finished wowing them.

- If it's conducting an important staff-meeting, see yourself taking charge and crushing that meeting. Imagine in detail exactly what you plan on saying, how you will say it, and think what you will say in response to other attendees at the meeting.

- If it's presenting a sales presentation to a client, see yourself giving a perfect sales presentation. Imagine also, every objection that might come your way, and see yourself handling those objections with grace and confidence.

- If it's approaching that beautiful girl at the coffee shop, imagine yourself striking up a conversation confidently, and holding a great engaging conversation with the person. Imagine everything that could go right.

APPENDIX C:

EXPERIMENT 2: THOUGHT EXPERIMENT

Below is a thought experiment that one can take to deconstruct their fears, so as to minimize worries and escape paralysis. Although this is a thought experiment, best results may come from writing it down.

- Define that which is causing you fear. Think in detail, exactly what it is you are so afraid of. Jot it down.

- Then, once you've defined your fear, consider what the worst possible outcome would be, if you did that thing which you are so afraid of doing. Jot it down.

- After you've come up with the answer(s), and have written them down, start to imagine exactly what you would do to 'dust yourself off', after that worse-case scenario happened? Start with the simple steps that you would take to get back on track.

- Now ask yourself "What are the big benefits that I will experience, if I do this thing I fear?".

- Next, ask yourself, "What will it cost me (short-term, long-term, physically, spiritually, mentally, monetarily), if I don't do this thing which I fear?"

- Finally, the last thing to ask yourself, after you've written down all the other responses, is "What am I waiting for?".[14]

APPENDIX D: CALENDAR

The following calendar was included to help you hold yourself accountable to using your fearless formula consistently.

The best way to use it is to simply mark every day on the calendar that you practiced using any antidotes of your formula. As mentioned in the 'how to use this formula' section of this resource, forcing yourself to use various aspects of this formula for at least **66 days** consistently, will considerably condition your ability to increase your confidence levels and be more fearless long-term.

On the next few pages you will find calendars that you can mark up, to signal the days you practiced using some of the fearless formula antidotes.

Note: By marking the number of the antidote you practiced the day you practiced, can lead to clues for which one worked best for you.

For example, you may mark a 1, and a 4 on Tuesday, and a 6 on all the other days, but noticed you felt at your best, and most fearless on the days you practiced antidotes 1 and 4. Having such insight can help you learn what antidotes are working best for you over time. This will allow you to use what works and discard what doesn't.

APPENDIX D:

MONTH 1

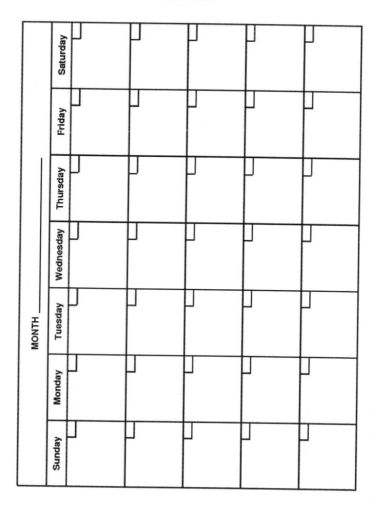

APPENDIX D:

MONTH 2

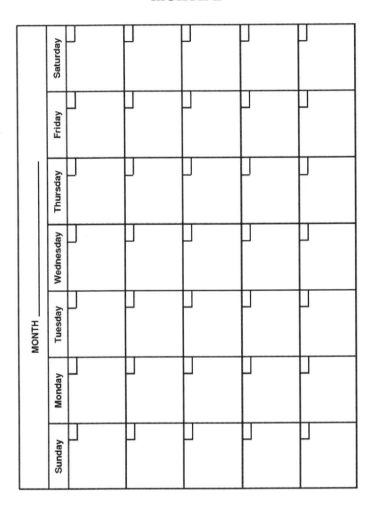

APPENDIX D:

MONTH 3

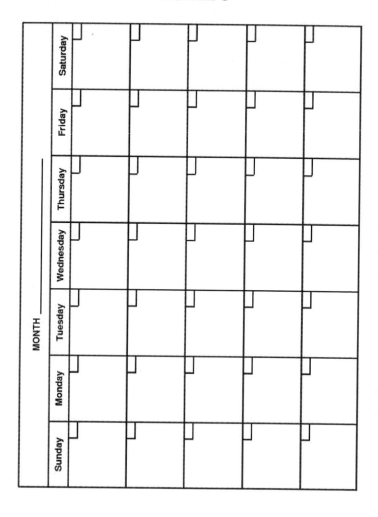

APPENDIX D:

Note: If you are interested in using a more high-tech means to track your progress, I recommend using a simple app like Habit List. You can visit their site at www.habitlist.com, and they have a pretty powerful app for $3 - $5 that is extremely helpful in tracking progress towards a goal, or towards creating a habit.

THE END: THE FEARLESS DECLARATION

There is nothing stronger than declaring to one's self your commitment to seeing something through.

Doing so can create the level of certainty and confidence needed to help us take the positive action required to conquer our fears.

As such, a fearless declaration page has been placed on the following page. It is suggested that you fill it out with sincerity and conviction, and then come back to it often. Taking this step will help remind you of your commitment towards becoming fearless.

This step has been intentionally placed at the end of the book. It is meant to serve both as a reminder of your completion of your fearless formula, and of your commitment to conquering your fears, so you can conquer life.

(See Next Page for Your Fearless Declaration)

THE
FEARLESS DECLARATION

I _____ declare, here and now, that I am committed to conquering my fears. I know that fear is the thief of humanity's light, and that if left unchecked it will seek to negatively alter the plans I have for my life.

As such, I choose today, to drive my fears into a corner, so that my desires for success may be actualized, and my personal greatness can be realized.

I realize that fear is nothing but the human motive of aversion, with its sole aim being an immediate release from threat, strain, or pain. Unless facing physical harm or death, I will no longer be afraid. I will stop fleeing from myself. I will stop fleeing from emotional discomfort at the expense of **MY GREATNESS**.

I am deciding today, to recognize that **I am** the **master of my fears**, and consequently the **master of my fate**.

Signature _____ **Fearless Since (Date)** _____

ABOUT THE AUTHOR

NATE LEE MORALES

Nate is an author, entrepreneur, and artist, dedicated to helping people strive to live their greatest life, and accelerate their ability to become the person they aspire to be. Nate is constantly researching the strategies, tools, motivation and mindset hacks of the successful, and distills his findings on the **TheStrive.co** platform.

Nate is the Founder of **The STRIVE**, a self-improvement and motivational website for strivers, dreamers, and go-getters: with articles on fitness, self-discipline, becoming fearless, making money, staying fired-up to become better, and living life to its fullest.

OTHER RECOMMENDED RESOURCES

Courage: The Joy of Living Dangerously
By Osho

Feel the Fear and Do It Anyway
By Susan Jeffers, Ph.D

End the Struggle and Dance with Life
By Susan Jeffers, Ph.D

The Magic of Thinking Big
By David J. Schwartz, Ph.D

Think and Grow Rich
By Napoleon Hill

The Motivation Manifesto
By Brendon Burchard

How to Stop Worrying and Start Living
By Dale Carnegie

Mastery
By Robert Greene

SELECTED BILIOGRAPHY

Antidotes 1 – 8:

1. Brendon Burchard, The Motivation Manifesto (Carlsbad: Hay House, 2014), 26.

2. Susan Jeffers Ph.D., Feel The Fear and Do It Anyway (New York: Ballantine Books, 2007), 22.

3. David J. Schwartz Ph.D., The Magic of Thinking Big (New York: Prentice Hall, 1965), 52.

4. Susan Jeffers, Feel The Fear and Do It Anyway (New York: Ballantine Books, 2007), 36.

5. Napoleon Hill, Think and Grow Rich (New York: Penguin Group, 2005), 52,53.

6. Napoleon Hill, Think and Grow Rich (New York: Penguin Group, 2005), 54.

7. Ronald Alexander, Ph.D., 5 Steps to Make Affirmations Work For You

(PsychologyToday.com. 2011),
https://www.psychologytoday.com/blog/the-wise-open-mind/201108/5-steps-make-affirmations-work-you

8. Susan Jeffers Ph.D., Feel The Fear and Do It Anyway (New York: Ballantine Books, 2007), 26.

SELECTED BIBLIOGRAPHY

Antidote 9 - Ted Talk Videos:

9. Ted.com: Video 1:
https://www.ted.com/talks/amy_cuddy_your_body_language_shapes_who_you_are

10 Ted.com: Video 2:
https://www.ted.com/talks/tim_ferriss_smash_fear_learn_anything

11 Ted.com: Video 3:
https://www.ted.com/talks/joe_kowan_how_i_beat_stage_fright

12. Ted.com: Video 4:
https://www.ted.com/talks/jia_jiang_what_i_learned_from_100_days_of_rejection

Antidote 10 – Follow Your Fire

13. Robert Greene, Mastery (New York: Penguin Group, 2012), 13,14.

Mental Exercises:

14. Tim Ferris, Tools of Titans (New York: Houghton Mifflin Harcourt, 2017), 468.

DISCLAIMER

The information contained in this guide is for informational purposes only. Any advice that I give is my opinion based on my own experience. You should always seek the advice of a professional before acting on something that I have published or recommended.

The material in this guide may include information, products, or services by third parties. Third Party Materials comprise the products and opinions expressed by their owners. As such, I do not assume responsibility or liability for any Third-Party material or opinions.

The publication of such Third-Party Materials does not constitute my guarantee of any information, instruction, opinion, products, or services contained within the Third-Party Material. The use of recommended Third-Party Material does not guarantee any success related to you or your business. Publication of such Third-Party Material is simply a recommendation and an expression of my own opinion of that material.

No part of this publication shall be reproduced, transmitted, or sold in whole or in part in any form, without the prior written consent of the author. All trademarks and registered trademarks appearing in this guide are the property of their respective owners. Users of this guide are advised to do their own due diligence when it comes to making business decisions and all information, products, and services that have been provided should be independently verified by your own qualified professionals. By reading this guide, you agree that myself and my company is not responsible for the success or failure of your business decisions relating to any information presented in this guide.

NOTES

NOTES

NOTES

NOTES

Printed in the United States of America

CATALOG:
Morales, Nate Lee

   Go Fearless/Nate Lee Morales
p. cm.

First Edition
Interior Designed by: Strive Industries, LLC

THE STRIVE.co
Strive Industries LLC.

Made in the USA
Middletown, DE
13 February 2018